U.S. WARS

THE PERSIAN GULF WAR

A MyReportLinks.com Book

Henry M. Holden

MyReportLinks.com Books
an imprint of
 Enslow Publishers, Inc. **E**
Box 398, 40 Industrial Road
Berkeley Heights, NJ 07922
USA

MyReportLinks.com Books, an imprint of Enslow Publishers, Inc. MyReportLinks is
a trademark of Enslow Publishers, Inc.

Library of Congress Cataloging-in-Publication Data

Holden, Henry M.
  The Persian Gulf War / Henry M. Holden.
    p. cm. — (U.S. wars)
Summary: Discusses the military tactics, battles, and famous figures of
the Persian Gulf War.
Includes bibliographical references and index.
  ISBN 0-7660-5109-9
  1. Persian Gulf War, 1991—Juvenile literature. [1. Persian Gulf War,
1991.] I. Title. II. Series.
  DS79.723 .H65 2003
  956.7044'2—dc21
                            2002003421

Printed in the United States of America

10 9 8 7 6 5 4 3 2 1

To Our Readers:
Through the purchase of this book, you and your library gain access to the Report Links that specifically back up this book.
The Publisher will provide access to the Report Links that back up this book and will keep these Report Links up to date on **www.myreportlinks.com** for three years from the book's first publication date.
We have done our best to make sure all Internet addresses in this book were active and appropriate when we went to press. However, the author and the Publisher have no control over, and assume no liability for, the material available on those Internet sites or on other Web sites they may link to.
The usage of the MyReportLinks.com Books Web site is subject to the terms and conditions stated on the Usage Policy Statement on **www.myreportlinks.com**.
In the future, a password may be required to access the Report Links that back up this book. The password is found on the bottom of page 4 of this book.
Any comments or suggestions can be sent by e-mail to comments@myreportlinks.com or to the address on the back cover.

Photo Credits: © Corel Corporation, pp. 1 (background), 3; AP/Wide World Photos, p. 17; CNN.com, pp. 18, 26; Department of Defense, pp. 1, 13, 24, 28, 29, 31, 33, 34, 36, 40; Gulflink, p. 42; MyReportLinks.com Books, p. 4; National Archives and Records Administration, p. 22; *Soldiers Online*, The Official Magazine of The United States Army, p. 39; SR-71 Online, p. 11; The Perry Castañeda Map Collection, The University of Texas Libraries, pp. 16, 21.

Cover Photo: © Corel Corporation

Contents

MyReportLinks.com Books
Great Books, Great Links, Great for Research!

MyReportLinks.com Books present the information you need to learn about your report subject. In addition, they show you where to go on the Internet for more information. The pre-evaluated Report Links that back up this book are kept up to date on **www.myreportlinks.com**. With the purchase of a MyReportLinks.com Books title, you and your library gain access to the Report Links that specifically back up that book. The Report Links save hours of research time and link to dozens—even hundreds—of Web sites, source documents, and photos related to your report topic.

Please see "To Our Readers" on the Copyright page for important information about this book, the MyReportLinks.com Books Web site, and the Report Links that back up this book.

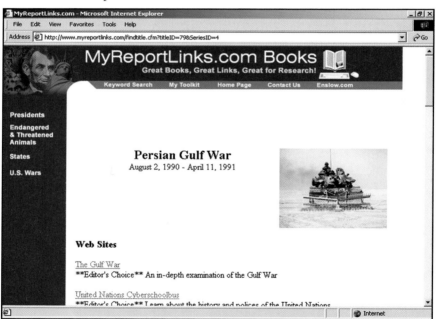

Access:

The Publisher will provide access to the Report Links that back up this book and will try to keep these Report Links up to date on our Web site for three years from the book's first publication date. Please enter **UGW5699** if asked for a password.

Report Links

➤ The Internet sites described below can be accessed at
http://www.myreportlinks.com

*EDITOR'S CHOICE

▶ **The Gulf War**

This PBS Web site provides an in-depth examination of the Gulf War.
Here you will find interviews with major decision makers and key
players, accounts from prisoners of war, photos, and information about
weaponry and technology used in the war.

Link to this Internet site from http://www.myreportlinks.com

*EDITOR'S CHOICE

▶ **United Nations Cyberschoolbus**

At this Web site you can learn about the history and policies of the
United Nations. You can also explore current events, view an interactive
map of United Nations member states, and read United Nations
core treaties.

Link to this Internet site from http://www.myreportlinks.com

*EDITOR'S CHOICE

▶ **The Unfinished War: A Decade Since Desert Storm**

This CNN Web site includes time lines of Operation Desert Storm.
It also features interviews with some of the people who participated in
the Gulf War and provides updated information on the war's legacy.

Link to this Internet site from http://www.myreportlinks.com

*EDITOR'S CHOICE

▶ **George Bush Presidential Library and Museum**

Take a virtual tour of the George Bush Presidential Library and
Museum. You will find biographies, photos, and related information
about America's president during the Gulf War.

Link to this Internet site from http://www.myreportlinks.com

*EDITOR'S CHOICE

▶ **Iraq Maps**

This site features maps of Iraq, including maps of cities in Iraq,
regional maps, thematic maps, historical maps, and links to other
map resources.

Link to this Internet site from http://www.myreportlinks.com

*EDITOR'S CHOICE

▶ **Operation Desert Storm**

This Web site provides statistics relating to Operation Desert Storm.
Find out why Iraqi troops surrendered by the thousands. You will also
find links to other reference sources on Operation Desert Storm.

Link to this Internet site from http://www.myreportlinks.com

Report Links

The Internet sites described below can be accessed at
http://www.myreportlinks.com

▶**A-10/OA-10 Thunderbolt II**

At this Web site you will learn about the A-10/OA-10 Thunderbolt II, used
in the Gulf War. These twin-engine Air Force aircraft were the first aircraft
specifically designed to support ground troops.

Link to this Internet site from http://www.myreportlinks.com

▶**Academy of Achievement**

At this Web site you can read a biography of Colin Powell, the first African
American to be appointed Chairman of the Joint Chiefs of Staff and later
secretary of state. You will also find photographs and a detailed interview
with Powell.

Link to this Internet site from http://www.myreportlinks.com

▶**Airpower in Operation Desert Storm**

Did you know the U.S. Air Force used space technology in Operation Desert
Storm? At this Web site you will learn about this and other weaponry and
technology used in the Gulf War.

Link to this Internet site from http://www.myreportlinks.com

▶**All POW—MIA From the Persian Gulf**

At this Web site you will find articles, documents, records, testimonies, and
reports relating to prisoners of the Gulf War. Also included are articles and
documents about Navy pilot Scott Speicher, whose fate is still unknown
and remains the center of debate today.

Link to this Internet site from http://www.myreportlinks.com

▶**The Battleship *Wisconsin* Foundation**

At the Battleship *Wisconsin* Web site you can take a virtual tour of the USS
Wisconsin, which participated in the Gulf War. Here you will learn about the
ship's dimensions, armaments, berthing, and about the foundation itself.

Link to this Internet site from http://www.myreportlinks.com

▶**The Canadian Way of War: The Legacy of Operation Friction
and the Gulf War**

This paper defines Canada's role in the Gulf War. Learn how Canada handled
the task of having to mobilize a naval and air presence when past military
history dictated ground force prominence.

Link to this Internet site from http://www.myreportlinks.com

Report Links

The Internet sites described below can be accessed at
http://www.myreportlinks.com

▶ **CIA Support to the U.S. Military During the Persian Gulf War**
One of the CIA's primary functions is to provide intelligence support to United States military forces. Learn what types of information the CIA passed along that helped the military to plan its strategy in the Gulf War.
Link to this Internet site from http://www.myreportlinks.com

▶ **Gulflink: Gulf War Illnesses**
This site is provided by the Department of Defense's Office of the Special Assistant for Gulf War Illnesses. It offers a library of ongoing government research into the illnesses suffered by the men and women who served in the Persian Gulf War.
Link to this Internet site from http://www.myreportlinks.com

▶ **Extended Iraq Coverage**
At this Web site you will find dozens of articles relating to Saddam Hussein and the Gulf War. You will also find time lines and learn about weapons used in the war.
Link to this Internet site from http://www.myreportlinks.com

▶ **Flashback: The Gulf War**
At this Web site you will find articles and interactive maps relating to the Gulf War. You will also learn about the military defenses of Iraq and those of the United States.
Link to this Internet site from http://www.myreportlinks.com

▶ **Gulf War Photographs**
At this Web site you can view photographs of Desert Storm taken by U.S. Army personnel. There are thirteen galleries to choose from.
Link to this Internet site from http://www.myreportlinks.com

▶ **How Night Vision Works**
Ever wonder how night vision works? It was essential to the pilots who conducted nighttime bombing raids during the Gulf War. This site explains the technology that enables pilots and others to see things more clearly in the dark.
Link to this Internet site from http://www.myreportlinks.com

Report Links

The Internet sites described below can be accessed at
http://www.myreportlinks.com

▶**Iraq**
The State Department Web site provides an analysis of human rights under the rule of Saddam Hussein in Iraq. This report focuses on the repression of Iraq's people, their lack of freedom, discrimination against women, and workers' rights.

Link to this Internet site from http://www.myreportlinks.com

▶**Military.com**
At this Web site you will find a brief biography of General H. Norman Schwarzkopf, the commander of the Allied coalition forces in the Persian Gulf War. The site includes a list of the medals awarded to the general and some interesting quotations.

Link to this Internet site from http://www.myreportlinks.com

▶*The Washington Post:* **Fog of War**
This *Washington Post* Web site presents a comprehensive picture of the Persian Gulf War and includes interviews, images, and analyses. Photos of some of the damage inflicted upon Iraqi targets are also included.

Link to this Internet site from http://www.myreportlinks.com

▶**Newsmakers: Saddam Hussein**
ABC News provides a brief biography of Saddam Hussein. Here you will learn about his birthplace, education, and political beliefs. You will also find a link to current articles about him.

Link to this Internet site from http://www.myreportlinks.com

▶**Operation Granby—The Gulf War 1991**
At this British Web site you can read official reports of the Royal Air Force's involvement in the Gulf War. Also included are a day-by-day history, a photo gallery, background information, squadron history, and links to other sources.

Link to this Internet site from http://www.myreportlinks.com

▶**The Program in Presidential Rhetoric—TAMU**
At this Web site you can read a speech given by President George H.W. Bush weeks after the first strikes against Iraq. In the speech, Bush discusses what prompted the strikes and talks about the budget crisis of the time.

Link to this Internet site from http://www.myreportlinks.com

Report Links

➤ The Internet sites described below can be accessed at
http://www.myreportlinks.com

▶ SR-71 Online—F-117A Nighthawk
Learn about the F-117A Nighthawk aircraft, also known as the stealth
fighter, which was used in combat during the Gulf War. Several photos
are available along with specifications of the aircraft.

Link to this Internet site from http://www.myreportlinks.com

▶ Saddam Hussein's Iraq
Saddam Hussein's Iraq, a report prepared by the United States
Department of State, presents facts about the current situation in Iraq.
The subjects discussed in this report include the impact of sanctions
on Iraq, repression of the Iraqi people, Iraq's failure to disarm, and
war crimes.
Link to this Internet site from http://www.myreportlinks.com

▶ The United Service Organizations
America's Story from America's Library, a Library of Congress Web site,
provides a brief history of the United Service Organizations, which
initially provided recreation for U.S. military on leave. Here you will
learn about many of the entertainers who have entertained U.S. troops
at home and abroad.
Link to this Internet site from http://www.myreportlinks.com

▶ Virginia War Museum
At the Virginia War Museum you can view pictures and read
specifications of the M60 Battle Tank, which was used in the Gulf War.

Link to this Internet site from http://www.myreportlinks.com

▶ Women in the Army: A Proud History
It was just after the Gulf War that women serving in the U.S. armed
forces were allowed to fly combat missions. But did you know that
women have long been a part of U.S. military history? This article
tells of women's roles in the military from the Revolutionary War to
the present.
Link to this Internet site from http://www.myreportlinks.com

▶ 5th Allied POW Squadron
The 5th Allied POW Squadron was formed at the end of the Gulf War
by former Allied prisoners of war. The squadron's site not only
educates the public about the experiences of Gulf War POWs but also
serves as a forum for the former prisoners of war to keep in touch with
each other. Link to this Internet site from http://www.myreportlinks.com

Persian Gulf War Facts

1990—*Aug. 2:* Iraq invades Kuwait.

—*Aug. 7:* Operation Desert Shield: first U.S. forces arrive in Saudi Arabia.

—*Nov. 29:* UN Security Council authorizes use of "all means necessary" to eject Iraq from Kuwait and passes Resolution 678, which sets a January 15, 1991, deadline for Iraq to withdraw its forces from Kuwait.

1991—*Jan. 12:* Congress authorizes use of force in Persian Gulf.

—*Jan. 15:* U.N. deadline for Iraqi withdrawal passes.

—*Jan. 17:* Operation Desert Storm begins with Allied air attack; Iraq launches first Scud missiles at Israel.

—*Feb. 23:* Bush sets deadline of noon for Iraqi withdrawal.

—*Feb. 24:* Allied ground assault begins.

—*Feb. 25:* Iraq launches Scud missile at U.S. barracks in Dhahran, Saudi Arabia; 28 American soldiers are killed.

—*Feb. 26:* Iraqis flee Kuwait City.

—*Feb. 28:* A "cessation of hostilities" is declared.

—*March 1:* Terms of cease-fire are negotiated in Safwan, Iraq.

—*March 5:* POWs released.

—*April 6:* Iraq accepts the U.N. cease-fire.

—*April 11:* U.N. cease-fire takes effect.

—*June 8:* Victory parade in Washington, D.C.

▶ Statistics

Allied coalition

34 countries including the United States, Great Britain, France, Italy, Egypt, and a Joint Arab Task Force.

American troops involved: 541,000; *Coalition troops:* 254,000.

American casualties: 148 battle deaths; 145 nonbattle deaths. *Coalition forces:* 92 deaths.

American wounded: 467; *Coalition:* 318[1]

Allied prisoners of war: 45 (21 Americans).
Women killed: 15.

Allied combat air sorties flown: more than 116,000.

Iraq

Casualties: 35,000[2]

Wounded: 300,000

Deserted: 650,000 (estimated)

Prisoners of war: 71,204 taken prisoner and released to Saudi control.

Fire in the Skies: January 17, 1991

At twenty-two minutes after midnight, on January 17, 1991, ten bat-winged F-117A stealth fighters code-named "Thunder" took off from Khamis Mushait, in Saudi Arabia.[1] Their mission was to bomb Iraqi bridges, air defenses, communications sites, and power plants. At 2:30 A.M. they refueled their tanks from an aerial tanker,

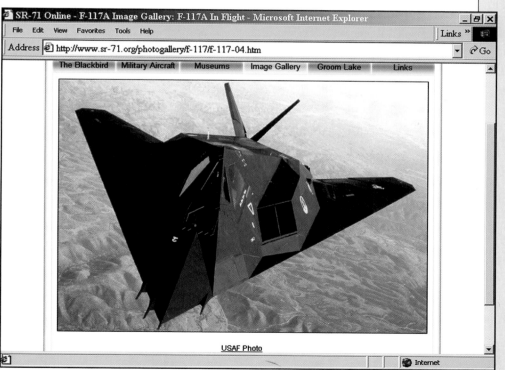

SR-71 Online - F-117A Image Gallery: F-117A In Flight - Microsoft Internet Explorer

File   Edit   View   Favorites   Tools   Help

Links »

Address http://www.sr-71.org/photogallery/f-117/f-117-04.htm

Go

The Blackbird   Military Aircraft   Museums   Image Gallery   Groom Lake   Links

USAF Photo

Internet

▲ An F-117A Nighthawk. These U.S. Air Force stealth fighter planes, designed to be difficult for enemy radar to detect, led the bombing missions over Iraq in Operation Desert Storm.

replacing the fuel they had used. About twenty minutes later, flying at close to 650 miles per hour, they would drop the first bombs of Operation Desert Storm, in what has come to be called the Persian Gulf War. Desert Storm was an attack on Iraq by a United States–led coalition of forces after Iraq had invaded Kuwait, its small neighbor to the southeast.

The targets were just outside Baghdad, Iraq, and easy to find on the plane's radar. Since the F-117 stealth fighters are almost invisible to radar, there was no antiaircraft fire coming up from Baghdad.

After finding the target, Colonel Greg Feest, an F-117 pilot, aimed the crosshairs of his weapon system on the bridge. He pressed a button on his control stick, and the computers took over.

"My laser began to fire as I tracked the target," said Feest. "I waited for the display to tell me I was 'in range,' and I depressed the 'pickle' button." The pickle button is a nickname for the bomb release. "Several seconds later the weapons bay door snapped open, and I felt the 2,000-pound bomb depart the aircraft. . . . I saw the bomb go through the crosshairs and penetrate the bunker . . . I knew I had knocked out the target. The video game was over."[2]

▶ Apaches in the Air

As the stealth fighters approached Baghdad, six helicopters were tearing through the night sky. They were about seventy-five feet above the dark sand of the Great Nafud Desert, in Saudi Arabia. They were racing single file toward the border with Iraq, to destroy Iraqi radar sites.

Leading four Army AH-64 Apache helicopter gunships were two Air Force MH-53J Pave Low helicopters, chock-full of complex navigation equipment. They were the "pathfinders," responsible for locating the target for the

Apaches. The four Apaches were loaded with rockets, missiles, and extra fuel tanks.

The night air over the desert was cold, and the heater in the lead helicopter was not working. Sand prevented the pilot, Warrant Officer Thomas R. "Tip" O'Neal, from closing some valves. From the backseat, his co-pilot, Warrant Officer David A. Jones, suddenly came on the intercom. "Tip, you see that glow off to the north? That might be it."[3]

O'Neal was wearing night-vision goggles, which help pilots see at night. The goggles intensify the light from the moon, stars, and ground. When wearing them, pilots do not see as if it were daylight. Instead, they see everything in pale green.

O'Neal saw the green glow in the distance. But he knew it was not the target, since they were still thirty miles from the radar site.

▲ Army AH-64 Apache helicopters destroyed enemy radar sites, among other targets, during the Gulf War. General Norman Schwarzkopf hailed the Apache pilots, saying they "plucked out the eyes" of Iraq's air defense systems.

Suddenly O'Neal's goggles filled with small starbursts of light. It was gunfire from the ground. Jones peered into the Apache's forward-looking infrared scope, which could "see" heat rather than visible light. Suddenly red tracer bullets that looked like tracks of fire poured from the Pave Low in front of them. The Pave Low was shooting back.

It was just after 2:00 A.M. The border lay behind them now. The attack plan called for the Pave Lows to lead the Apaches directly toward the target. They would fly just above the desert floor, to hide their movement from the enemy's radar.

Twelve miles from the target, the Pave Lows dropped two bundles of chemical sticks. They glowed like green coals as they fell. They were a signal to the Apaches that they were now close enough to find their own way. The Pave Lows slipped sideways, allowing the Apaches to continue moving ahead. They hovered for a short time, and then they headed back to Saudi Arabia.

The Apache pilots began to line up for the attack. The helicopters shifted left and right in battle-spread formation. They flew in a formation of four across toward the green glow that was growing larger ahead of them.[4] They would unleash their rockets and missiles and destroy the radar sites. General Norman Schwarzkopf, the American general in charge of Operation Desert Storm, praised the efforts of the Army Apaches, saying that they "plucked out the eyes" of Iraq's air defenses.[5]

For the next forty-three days, the Allied air forces would pound Iraqi targets. Then Allied troops on the ground would fight for only one hundred hours before the Persian Gulf War came to an end.

Prelude to War: A History of Iraq

The Middle Eastern nation of Iraq, at the head of the Arabian Peninsula, was once part of Mesopotamia, the world's earliest known civilization. Over the centuries, Mesopotamia was conquered by many groups, including the Persians, Greeks, Arabs, Mongols, and Turks. After World War I, new political boundaries were drawn in many parts of the world, including the Middle East. Mesopotamia, which had been invaded by Great Britain during World War I, was ruled by it for a time afterward. It was while the country was under British rule that it was renamed Iraq.

In 1922, the British recognized Iraq as a kingdom and determined Iraq's border with its tiny neighbor Kuwait. That new border greatly diminished Iraq's coastline on the Persian Gulf. British rule of Iraq ended in 1932, and Iraq established its independence as a monarchy.[1] By 1943, during World War II, Iraq allied itself with the Axis powers. In 1945, Iraq was one of the founding members of the Arab League. The league, an organization of Arab countries, participated in a war against the newly formed state of Israel in 1948.

Army officers overthrew the Iraqi government in 1958, and the country was declared a republic. In 1968, the radical Ba'ath Party, which sought to make Iraq an Islamic empire, came into power. A member of that party was a thirty-one-year-old man named Saddam Hussein. Hussein quickly rose through the ranks to become the government's ruthless security chief.

▶ The Rise of Saddam Hussein

Hussein, who was born on April 28, 1937, in Tikrit, came from a poor family. He joined the Ba'ath Party when he was only twenty years old. In 1958, he and other party members attempted to assassinate Iraq's military dictator. In 1979 the Iraqi military leader who had named Saddam Hussein his security chief eleven years earlier resigned.

▲ Iraq. Tikrit, Hussein's hometown, is 100 miles north of Baghdad.

▲ *Saddam Hussein, Iraq's president for more than twenty years, was defeated in the Persian Gulf War, but he remains in power—and with him, so does the threat that he will use weapons of mass destruction to attain his ends.*

Hussein grabbed control. He became the president of the Republic of Iraq.

▶ A Ruthless Command

Iraq was, and continues to be, however, a republic in name only. Saddam Hussein rules as a dictator, seizing lands and killing opponents. In just his first week in power, Hussein had more than 500 Iraqi government and military officials executed by firing squad. And his desire to extend Iraq's boundaries and to gain more control over the region's oil supply led to an eight-year war with Iran, Iraq's neighbor to the west.

The Unfinished War: A Decade Since Desert Storm

MAIN

Inside Iraq

- Quiet reflection,
  business as usual mark
  anniversary in Baghdad

- Not much celebrating
  as anniversary
  approaches

- Saddam claims victory
  in Gulf War

The Unfinished War

- A Decade Since Desert
  Storm

- Intent vs. effect

- Uprisings and coups

- UNSCOM and Desert
  Fox

- The survival of Saddam
  Hussein

Keeping the Kurds safe

After the war, the allies began protecting what Saddam sought to destroy

(CNN) -- Before the Gulf War, Iraqi President Saddam Hussein conducted a campaign of suppression in the 1980s against the Kurd people living in northern Iraq, including a March 1988 poison gas attack in Halabja, Iraq, in which an estimated 5,000 Kurds were killed.

The Gulf War itself proved to be a momentary lull in Hussein's war against Kurds in northern Iraq. The Kurds were emboldened by the allies' victory in the war and used that victory to assert their own case for independence, but they were quickly defeated by the Iraqi armed forces. The offensive resulted in some 1.5 million Kurds scrambling through the mountains, headed for Turkey. The United Nations created what it called a "safe haven" in northern Iraq. Since the end of the Gulf War, U.S. and British military forces have enforced a "no-fly" zone over northern Iraq. This restricted zone was created to prevent Iraqi attacks against the Kurds. A similar zone in the South is meant to protect Shiite Muslims.

The U.N. also set up a humanitarian relief campaign, called Operation Provide Comfort. It officially began on April 7, 1991, when four U.S. Air Force C-130s took off from an airbase in Turkey to airdrop food and water to Kurdish refugees in northern Iraq.

Although the first phase of the operation ended in July 1991, the second phase began that same month and lasted for five more years. The U.S. armed forces, and other allies, flew more than 60,000 flights into the area, not only dropping off supplies but also patrolling for hostile aircraft.

Internet

▲ *In March 1988, Saddam Hussein used poison gas in an attack against the Kurds. Following the Allied victory in the Gulf War, the Kurds again tried to assert their independence, but were quickly defeated by the Iraqi Army. The United Nations set up a relief campaign to help Kurdish refugees who had fled to Turkey. And military forces of the United States and Great Britain continue to enforce a "no-fly zone" over northern Iraq to protect the Kurds still living there.*

▶ The Iran-Iraq War

That war, which lasted from 1980 to 1988, cost Iraq billions of dollars and the loss of many lives. Hussein's ruthlessness extended to his own people. In 1988, Hussein used poison gas against the Kurds, an ethnic minority living in northern Iraq, to crush a rebellion.

In 1990, Saddam Hussein then asked neighboring oil-rich countries Kuwait and Saudi Arabia to help him bear some of the costs of Iraq's war with Iran. He justified his request by saying that his army—the world's fourth largest at the time—had protected those countries from Iran. He also asked them to cut oil production to help raise the price of oil, which they refused to do. Iraq's economy, like many of the economies in the Persian Gulf region, is dependent on revenues from oil. And he finally accused Kuwait of stealing oil from Iraq by slant drilling, drilling under Iraq into the Rumaila oil field. That oil field lay in the northern part of Kuwait and the southern part of Iraq.

When Kuwait failed to decrease its oil production and would not agree to stop drilling on lands Hussein claimed were Iraq's, Hussein massed his troops along the border with Kuwait.

Chapter 3 ▶

The Buildup: Operation Desert Shield

On August 2, 1990, the people of Kuwait City awoke to the sounds of Iraqi tanks rumbling through their streets. Kuwait's small army was no match for Iraq, as the Iraqi army troops rolled through the country. The Iraqis were also massed along Kuwait's southern border with Saudi Arabia. An attack on Saudi Arabia's oil fields could be launched easily.

World leaders feared that Hussein might attack Saudi Arabia next, leading to a large and bloody war. Israeli leaders worried that Iraq would launch missiles at Israel. The rest of the world feared they might be the targets of terrorists' attacks. And there was concern that Hussein's actions might prompt other dictators to think they could invade their neighbors and get away with it.

The United Nations condemned the invasion, but rejected any quick military action against Iraq. Instead, the United Nations placed economic sanctions on Iraq, which meant that Iraq could not import things like food and medicine that it desperately needed. The sanctions also prevented Iraq from selling its oil, which meant Iraq would lose a lot of money. The sanctions caused great hardship for the Iraqi people but did not cause Hussein to withdraw his forces.

▶ Operation Desert Shield

The United States and other world powers knew that Iraq's actions were a threat to oil production in the region, since Kuwait at the time produced about 20 percent of the world's oil. That oil was now in the hands of Hussein, and a worldwide oil shortage might result. On August 6, Saudi Arabia's ruler, King Fahd, gave the United States president George Bush permission to move American troops into Saudi Arabia. The Saudis had an army of only about 28,000 men and welcomed the help of the United States in defending their nation from possible invasion. Within two weeks, there were about 30,000 American troops in

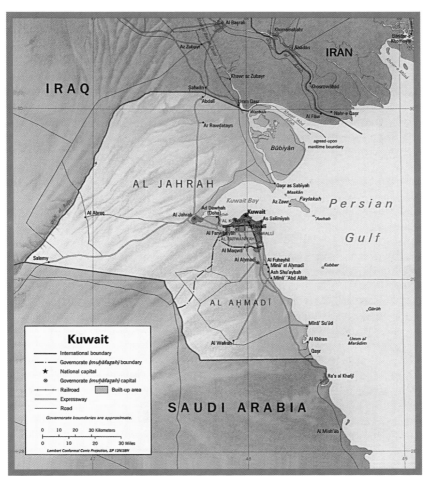

▲ This relief map of Kuwait shows its flat desert landscape.

Saudi Arabia. It would take thousands more troops, from many countries, to push Hussein out of Kuwait. Those troops would be part of a coalition force. The buildup of coalition forces and weapons in Saudi Arabia in response to Iraq's invasion of Kuwait was code-named Operation Desert Shield.

▶ Occupation by Terror

On August 8, Hussein declared that Kuwait belonged to Iraq. The United Nations accused Iraq of violating international law in its occupation of Kuwait and set up

▲ This photograph shows President Bush meeting with the emir of Kuwait at the White House on September 28, 1990, to discuss Iraq's occupation of Kuwait.

a naval blockade that stopped supplies from reaching Iraq. That day, President Bush announced that he was sending American troops to help the Saudi government defend itself.

On August 24, foreign embassies in Kuwait City were surrounded by Iraqi troops.[1] The Iraqis cut off the water and electricity used by those embassies. The United States embassy personnel refused to leave. They bolted the door and used water from the swimming pool to keep clean. The Iraqi troops then began rounding up Kuwaiti government workers. Some were beaten, and others were shot.[2]

Then the Iraqis took some American and European oil workers prisoner and sent them to military bases in Kuwait to act as "human shields." Hussein believed the coalition would not attack those bases if it meant killing their own people. Hussein would later set all these hostages free.

Crimes Against Kuwait

The situation in Kuwait grew worse. According to the Pentagon, there were about 360,000 Iraqi troops in Kuwait by September 18, 1990.[3] The Iraqi army began to steal from businesses and private homes in Kuwait's cities. They raped and murdered Kuwaiti citizens. The people of Kuwait began to flee their country, some escaping in cars, others on camels, and still others on foot. The Iraqi army hunted them down and killed many of them. The United Nations finally could not ignore these crimes and knew they would continue if Iraq invaded Saudi Arabia.

By mid-October, there were almost half a million American troops in Saudi Arabia. It was the largest American military force assembled since the Vietnam War.

▲ *Thanksgiving in the desert: President Bush, with General Schwarzkopf behind him to the right, speaking to American troops in Saudi Arabia during Operation Desert Shield just before Thanksgiving of 1990.*

The coalition was building a powerful army, with more than a million troops ready to fight.

▶ The Risk—Weapons of Mass Destruction

But the enemy the coalition faced was not just one that used conventional weapons. Iraq had chemical, biological, and nuclear weapons of mass destruction. Hussein had already used chemical weapons in Iraq's war with Iran, and he had used poison gas to kill 5,000 Kurds living in his own country. There was a concern, therefore, that Hussein might use chemical or biological weapons again. A British

officer said that if Iraq used chemical weapons, he would use a tactical nuclear weapon. The United States would not say, however, if it would use nuclear weapons against Iraq.[4]

A Deadline Is Set

While the United Nations was trying to get Hussein out of Kuwait without resorting to war, the United States was preparing to bomb military targets in Iraq if the situation in the Persian Gulf remained unchanged or became worse. The goal was to destroy Iraq's military power.

Despite the hardships endured by the Iraqi people because of the U.N. sanctions, Hussein would not withdraw his forces. On November 29, the United Nations passed Resolution 678. It set January 15, 1991, as the deadline for Iraq to leave Kuwait. Time was running out for Saddam Hussein.

The Battle: Operation Desert Storm

On January 12, 1991, the United States Congress authorized President Bush to use military force to get Saddam Hussein out of Kuwait. The president had listed as the military's goals the removal of Iraq from Kuwait, the restoration of Kuwait's government, and the protection of American citizens and interests abroad.[1]

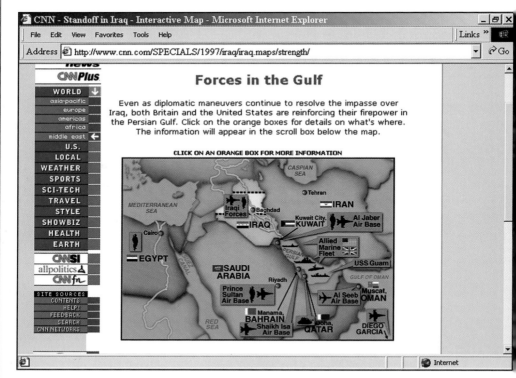

▲ While the United Nations continued it diplomatic efforts to end the Iraqi occupation of Kuwait, U.S. and British forces, together with other countries' forces, were mobilizing weapons and troops in the Persian Gulf region.

Antiwar Protests

Although many Americans supported a military action in the Gulf, antiwar protests erupted on college campuses even before the war began. Thousands of people protested at Duke University, in North Carolina. Thousands more marched at the University of Michigan. In California, students blocked traffic at the Golden Gate Bridge. Campus unrest was not nearly as great as it had been during the antiwar protests of the Vietnam War era, however. And not all the protesters were college students.

The media gave little notice to the protests. "Three days before we attacked Iraq, campuses across the country were exploding with resistance to the war," said Robin Templeton, of the National Coalition for Universities in the Public Interest. "The *New York Times* had no coverage of campus activism. Instead, the Sunday campus section had articles about students at MIT who had done experiments with M&Ms. . . ."[2]

There were no signs that the protests were a threat to the administration. After the beginning of air attacks, a *Newsweek* poll revealed that Americans showed a 5-to-1 support for military action.[3] The country was united in a way that it had never been during the long years of the Vietnam War.

Desert Storm Begins

On January 17, 1991, President George Bush ordered the United States Air Force to begin bombing military targets in Iraq. The air forces of coalition countries joined in the attack, which was code-named Operation Desert Storm. General H. Norman Schwarzkopf, the commander of the coalition forces, told his troops, "Our cause is just. Now you must be the thunder and lightning of Desert Storm."[4]

▶ The Generals in Charge: Schwarzkopf and Powell

H. Norman Schwarzkopf, Jr., was born on August 22, 1934, in Trenton, New Jersey. Schwarzkopf graduated from the United States Military Academy at West Point forty-third in a class of nearly five hundred. He then served two tours of duty in Vietnam for which he was awarded three Silver Stars, three Bronze Stars, and the Distinguished Service Medal. In 1970, Schwarzkopf had risked his life to save other soldiers in a minefield. In 1978, Schwarzkopf was made a general.

In 1988, General Schwarzkopf was made commander-in-chief of the United States Central Command. In that position, he was responsible for planning any military action that needed to be taken in nineteen Middle Eastern countries, including Saudi Arabia. The six-foot-three-inch, 240-pound general, who was well-respected by his troops, had earned the nickname "Stormin' Norman" from them for his quick and decisive actions.

General Norman Schwarzkopf, the commander-in-chief, U.S. Central Command, is pictured at Riyadh Air Base in Saudi Arabia as he waits to greet Allied prisoners of war released by Iraq.

General Colin Powell, the *Chairman of the Joint Chiefs of Staff, on the phone to the Pentagon during Operation Desert Shield. When asked at a news conference how the coalition planned to attack the Iraqi army, Powell was blunt: "Our strategy to go after this army is very, very simple. First, we're going to cut if off. And then we're going to kill it."*

As Chairman of the Joint Chiefs of Staff, General Colin Powell was the United States' top-ranking military leader. During the Gulf War, General Powell, who advised President Bush on all military matters, was responsible for all communications between the battlefield and the White House.

Colin Powell was born on April 5, 1937, in New York City, the son of Jamaican immigrants. He graduated from the City College of New York and George Washington University and then entered the United States Army in 1958. Like Schwarzkopf, Powell served two tours of duty in Vietnam. And also like Schwarzkopf, Powell performed heroic deeds in Vietnam. After the helicopter he was in crashed, he climbed back into the flames to save his commanding general and two other soldiers. Throughout his military career, Powell has been awarded two Purple Hearts, a Bronze Star, a Soldier's Medal, and the Legion of Merit.

Powell rose through the ranks of the service to become a four-star general and the first African American to be appointed Chairman of the Joint Chiefs of Staff. With Norman Schwarzkopf and Colin Powell, the coalition's leadership was in the hands of two battle-tested veterans.

Scuds and Patriots

Forty-eight hours after the bombing of Iraq began, air-raid sirens sounded throughout Israel. Scud missiles came raining down on two Israeli cities: Six missiles slammed into Tel Aviv, and two into Haifa. Scud missiles, first used by the Soviets in the 1960s, were designed to carry a nuclear warhead that could range between 100 and 180 miles. The coalition feared that the warheads had been adapted by Iraq to become chemical or biological weapons. So when Scud missiles were fired at Israel during the Persian Gulf War, the Israeli people put on gas masks and ran for bomb shelters. They had reason to fear that the missiles contained poison gas.

Iraq had fired the forty-foot-long Scud missiles at civilian targets because Saddam Hussein wanted to bring Israel into the war. If Israel entered the war, the Arab soldiers in the U.S.-led forces might leave, weakening the coalition. To keep Israel from striking back, the United States sent a new weapon, the Patriot missile, to Israel. The seventeen-foot-long Patriots were designed to intercept incoming Scuds and blow them apart before they could reach their targets.

In all, Iraq fired forty-one Scud missiles at Israel. The Patriot missiles destroyed most of them. Although several civilians were killed and hundreds injured, Israel did not go to war, and the coalition did not break up. The Israelis were not the only victims of Scud attacks, however. On

▲ *This photograph shows the remains of a warehouse that served as a U.S. Army barracks in Dhahran, Saudi Arabia, after Iraq fired a Scud missile at it on February 25, 1991. Twenty-eight U.S. Army Reserve personnel were killed in the attack, and nearly 100 were wounded.*

February 25, a Scud missile hit the U.S. Army barracks in Al Khobar (Dhahran), Saudi Arabia. Twenty-eight soldiers were killed and ninety-eight were wounded.⁶

▶ **The Four-Day Ground War**

Coalition warplanes continued to bomb Iraq for thirty-nine days. The bombs destroyed hundreds of Iraqi tanks and trucks and killed thousands of Iraqi soldiers. Iraq's military and industrial sites lay in ruins.

In spite of the widespread destruction of Iraq from the air, Hussein refused to pull his troops out of Kuwait. On

February 23, President Bush gave Hussein one last warning: Get out of Kuwait within twenty-four hours. The world held its breath. Hussein did not leave.

On February 24, the ground war began. General Schwarzkopf had assembled 18,000 Marines in the Persian Gulf, near the coast of Kuwait. Hussein, thinking the Marines were going to attack, placed thousands of Iraqi troops near the coast.

One hundred thousand American soldiers raced across the Iraqi desert from Saudi Arabia. Schwarzkopf's plan was to surround the enemy. U.S. Marines would attack from the south. Army troops would come in behind the enemy and trap them. With the beginning of the ground war, more than one thousand allied tanks smashed into the Iraqi army. They cut supply lines and escape routes from Kuwait.

The Iraqis were holed up deep in concrete bunkers. With artillery and tanks, they were expected to put up a fierce fight. Instead, thousands of Iraqi soldiers surrendered. Pounded by weeks of bombing, they were tired, hungry, and scared. Many of the drafted Iraqi soldiers thought they were going to die. There was little resistance to the ground attack.

▶ Scorched Earth and Black Tides

The Iraqi troops who did not surrender were in full retreat back to Iraq. Along the way, they destroyed billions of dollars in property in Kuwait. They purposely blew up oil wells and pipelines and set fire to 600 of Kuwait's 1,000 oil wells.[7] Reports estimated that $80 million a day in oil was burning in the desert. The smoke from those oil-well fires covered 1.3 million square miles.[8] Firefighters would use

▲ *This destroyed Iraqi tank sits atop the Basra-Kuwait Highway. It was hit during one of the final coalition attacks on the Iraqi army as it was trying to leave Kuwait City.*

millions of gallons of water to put out the fires. It would take five years before the oil fields were back to normal.

During the war, the Iraqis created the worst oil spill the world has ever seen by releasing more than 126 million gallons of oil from a pier off Kuwait. That was almost ten times the amount of oil spilled in the waters of Prince William Sound, Alaska, by the Exxon *Valdez* tanker in 1989, the largest oil spill in U.S. history.

The oil spill spread along the coastlines of Kuwait and Saudi Arabia for hundreds of miles. It nearly destroyed the Saudi shrimp industry and did kill thousands of seabirds, fish, plants, and other animals in the region.

▶ "Highway of Death"

On the night of February 24, U.S. spy planes spotted a large Iraqi convoy leaving Kuwait City.⁽¹⁰⁾ The military and civilian vehicles were loaded with Iraqi soldiers and goods stolen from Kuwait. Hundreds of tanks were in the convoy. The coalition's generals concluded that the Iraqi army might regroup and fight again, and they were considered a valid military target because they had firepower. President Bush said, "We have no choice but to treat the retreating combat units as a threat.⁽¹¹⁾ So to prevent the Iraqis from forming a new defense line, coalition warplanes bombed the convoy.

▲ The Marines after liberating Kuwait's airport, following the retreat of Iraqi troops.

It was night when the air force attacked the convoy. The convoy fired back with antiaircraft guns and heat-seeking missiles. The warplanes first destroyed the front of the convoy, to prevent it from moving forward. Then they destroyed the back of the convoy. They trapped more than a thousand vehicles. Many of the Iraqi troops fled.[12] In the morning, ground artillery and warplanes destroyed most of the vehicles.

When reporters reached the highway, they found total destruction. They called it the "highway of death." Photographs of charred bodies outraged human rights groups. But most of the vehicles on the highway were empty, and the casualty total was probably in hundreds and not thousands.[13] "Most of what existed on the so-called highway of death," said Bernard Trainor, a military analyst, "were stolen goods and stolen vehicles . . . Very few Iraqi solders were found amongst the wreckage."[14]

▶ Kuwait Is Liberated

By February 27, after only one hundred hours of ground fighting, the battle to free Kuwait was won. Iraq's Third Armored Division had been destroyed, and the U.S. and Arab forces had freed Kuwait's main airport and now controlled the roads that led into and out of Kuwait City. Members of the Arab coalition were then given the opportunity to liberate Kuwait City itself.

When General Powell heard of the destruction, he talked with General Schwarzkopf and then advised President Bush to call for a cease-fire. After six weeks of air strikes and one hundred hours of ground fighting, the Persian Gulf War was over.

Cease-fire and Aftermath

On February 27, 1991, President Bush ordered a cease-fire. Although it took effect the next day, the Iraqis did not honor it and engaged in fighting up until March 1. On that date, General Norman Schwarzkopf and a Saudi general met with two Iraqi lieutenant generals inside a tent at Safwan Air Field, in southern Iraq. The Iraqis were presented with the terms of the cease-fire and finally agreed to them.

▶ Objectives Achieved

The forty-three-day war was finally over, and it had achieved its objectives: Iraqi forces had been removed from

▲ *Presenting the terms of the cease-fire: General Schwarzkopf and Saudi Lieutenant General Khalid Aziz, the commander of the Joint Forces in Saudi Arabia, are seated across the table from two Iraqi lieutenant generals and an interpreter at Safwan Air Field.*

Kuwait, Iraq's military strength had been badly damaged, and the oil reserves of the Persian Gulf region had been preserved. President Bush said, "No one country can claim this victory as its own. It was not only a victory for Kuwait, but a victory for all the coalition partners. This is a victory for the United Nations, for all mankind, for the rule of law, and for what is right."[1]

Many of the American troops began leaving the region after the cease-fire. By late April 1991, the rest of the American troops left southern Iraq. A United Nations peacekeeping force was moved into Iraq's border with Kuwait, and Iraq was forced to agree to the destruction of its remaining chemical and biological weapons.

▶ An Incomplete Victory?

To most observers, the Persian Gulf War had been a one-sided battle and was considered a complete victory for the coalition. It ended, however, without a total surrender and with Saddam Hussein still in power. It had never been the Bush administration's stated goal to kill Saddam Hussein.[2] And President Bush declared that the fate of Hussein was up to the Iraqi people.[3]

Although many coalition members considered Hussein evil, they knew that killing him might not be wise. To some members of the Arab coalition, Hussein was considered a hero. It was feared that Hussein's death would upset the balance of power in the Middle East, maybe even leading to another, greater war. It was also believed that without Hussein, a civil war might start in Iraq. For many American citizens, however, the victory over Iraq was incomplete: A poll conducted after the cease-fire showed that 55 percent of the American public believed the war "should not have ended with Hussein still in power."[4]

▶ Outcome—The Good and the Bad

With such a decisive victory achieved, President Bush received high marks for his handling of the war. He did not, however, win reelection in 1992. An already weak U.S. economy was pushed into a recession, in which thousands of people lost their jobs. George Bush, whose popularity soared during and just after the war, was finally unable to convince the American people that the economy was recovering.

The war was a huge defeat for Hussein's military and it damaged Iraq's nuclear weapons programs. The United Nations established a group to make sure that Hussein destroyed those weapons. But in December 1998, Iraq refused to allow the U.N. weapons inspectors to inspect Iraqi weapons sites. In response, the United States and Great Britain launched Operation Desert Fox on December 17. This was four days of air strikes by U.S. and British air forces on Iraqi weapons facilities. The raids were the heaviest since Operation Desert Storm. But despite the reprisals, U.N. weapons inspectors are still being kept from Iraq's weapons sites.

▶ Gulf War Achievements—The Role of Women

Thirty-five thousand women served in the Persian Gulf War. They served in support roles, as air traffic controllers and noncombat pilots, because federal law barred them from combat. After the war, in the spring of 1991, Congresswoman Patricia Schroeder, a Democrat from Colorado, sponsored a bill to repeal the law that restricted women from flying combat missions. The bill passed, and the Army, Navy, and Air Force began training women in combat aircraft. The new law also extends to women serving on combat ships.[5]

Even though they did not see combat in the Gulf War, fifteen women died in the service of their country. And some women were taken as prisoners of war (POWs). U.S. Army flight surgeon Major Rhonda Cornum was one of them.

▶ Rhonda Cornum, POW

Rhonda Cornum found herself behind enemy lines during a search-and-rescue mission on February 27, 1991. She was aboard a helicopter looking for an F-16 pilot who had gone down.

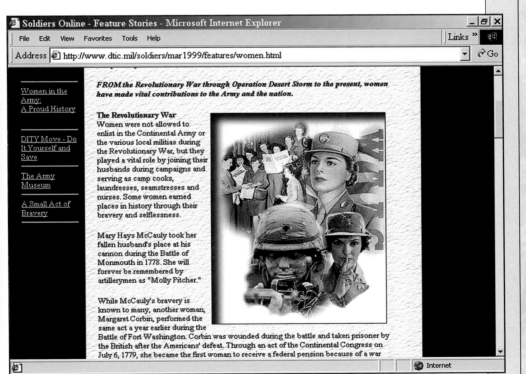

Soldiers Online - Feature Stories - Microsoft Internet Explorer

File　Edit　View　Favorites　Tools　Help

Links »

Address http://www.dtic.mil/soldiers/mar1999/features/women.html　　Go

Women in the Army:
A Proud History

DITY Move - Do It Yourself and Save

The Army Museum

A Small Act of Bravery

FROM the Revolutionary War through Operation Desert Storm to the present, women have made vital contributions to the Army and the nation.

The Revolutionary War
Women were not allowed to enlist in the Continental Army or the various local militias during the Revolutionary War, but they played a vital role by joining their husbands during campaigns and serving as camp cooks, laundresses, seamstresses and nurses. Some women earned places in history through their bravery and selflessness.

Mary Hays McCauly took her fallen husband's place at his cannon during the Battle of Monmouth in 1778. She will forever be remembered by artillerymen as "Molly Pitcher."

While McCauly's bravery is known to many, another woman, Margaret Corbin, performed the same act a year earlier during the Battle of Fort Washington. Corbin was wounded during the battle and taken prisoner by the British after the Americans' defeat. Through an act of the Continental Congress on July 6, 1779, she became the first woman to receive a federal pension because of a war

Internet

▲ The number of women who served in the military during Operation Desert Storm was unprecedented. But American women have been engaged in military service to their country since the American Revolution.

▲ Major Rhonda Cornum sitting next to an Army colonel aboard a transport aircraft after her release as a POW.

Some thirty minutes into the flight, bright green tracer bullets from unseen bunkers below began hitting the helicopter. The Black Hawk gunners fired back. It took just seconds for the Iraqis to blow off the helicopter's back end.

The helicopter smashed into sand at 150 miles per hour and burst into flames. "I remember thinking, 'at least I'm dying doing something honorable,'" said Cornum.[6] Then everything went black.

Cornum woke up and found herself pinned under the wreckage. It was dark and very quiet. "I was very comfortable, very peaceful," she said. "I had no desire to move. Nothing hurt as I lay motionless."[7]

As she tried to free herself, she saw five Iraqi soldiers pointing AK-47 assault rifles at her. "One of them, without saying anything, reached down and grabbed my right arm.

He pulled hard to get me up, and the pain shot through me and came out my mouth in a piercing scream."[8] Cornum knew that her arm was broken.

One of the Iraqi soldiers removed her pistol, flak vest, and helmet. Her long brown hair tumbled out. That is when they discovered she was a woman.

The soldiers then dragged Cornum to an underground bunker. "They threw me down next to somebody else," she said. It was Sergeant Troy Dunlap, one of the helicopter crew members. "That's when I knew there was another survivor."[9] She would later discover that a third crew member had survived.

Cornum recalled, "They just stood there, and they put their handguns to the back of our heads. We really thought they were gonna shoot us."[10] One of them pulled the trigger and the gun clicked on an empty chamber. The Iraqis were playing a sick game. "The only positive thing I could think of was, 'Well, it won't hurt.'"[11] Cornum had two broken arms, a bullet in her right shoulder, a broken finger, and a shattered knee.[12] There was no way for her to fight her captors.

The Iraqis took Cornum to a hospital in Baghdad, where she would remain with her injuries untreated for five days.[13] On the morning of March 5, 1991, an Iraqi soldier blindfolded her and told her she was leaving. He did not tell her where she was going. When her blindfold was finally removed, she was in a Baghdad hotel. The war now over, Cornum was finally safe—the Red Cross had arrived in Baghdad, and she was taken out of Iraq.

The Aftermath—Gulf War Syndrome

Nearly one sixth (more than 100,000) of the U.S. troops who served in the Persian Gulf War returned home with mysterious ailments. That figure is based on the number of veterans who registered their health complaints with either the Department of Veterans Affairs or the Department of Defense. The ailments they complained of include sleep disorders, joint pain, memory loss, rashes, and severe fatigue. In some cases, Gulf War veterans made it safely home from combat only to contract cancer.

The term "Gulf War Syndrome" has come to describe the undiagnosed illnesses suffered by Gulf War veterans. There have been many theories as to why so many veterans suffer from similar symptoms. More than ten years after

▲ More than 100,000 U.S. soldiers who fought in the Persian Gulf War returned home with a variety of lasting illnesses whose cause is yet to be determined. "Gulf War Syndrome" is the term that has come to be used for these undiagnosed ailments.

the war, however, no theory has been able to explain a link between the different ailments or a specific cause.

It is thought that repeated exposure to low levels of chemical agents, known as nerve agents, may have caused some of the ailments. Side effects from the vaccines and medicines that Gulf War participants received may also have played a part. Exposure to toxins released by the oil-well fires is another possibility. The federal government has funded more than 145 research studies to find the causes of—and thus better treatment for—the illnesses suffered by Gulf War veterans.[14]

The Legacy of Desert Storm

Iraq has been under U.N. sanctions since it invaded Kuwait in 1990. Those sanctions have been overhauled several times to lessen their impact on the Iraqi people and cause them less hardship. But since Saddam Hussein still refuses to admit U.N. weapons inspectors into Iraq, the sanctions have not been totally lifted.[15] More than twelve years after the Persian Gulf War, Hussein still controls Iraq and is believed to be stockpiling weapons of mass destruction.

The United States military still flies patrols over Iraq. They watch for any unfriendly action against the Iraqi people. They also watch for hostile movements toward Kuwait or Saudi Arabia.

In spite of the death and destruction brought about by the war, there were some positive outcomes. The United Nations proved to be a force in world politics, and the victory gave Americans a new sense of pride in their military. For the first time in more than forty years, American soldiers returned home from a war fought on foreign soil as heroes, and the nation was grateful.

Persian Gulf War Facts

1. The United States Department of Defense, *DefenseLINK News: The Operation Desert Shield/Desert Storm Timeline*, May 16, 2002, <www.defenselink.mil/news/Aug2000/n08082000 _20008088.html>.

2. Ibid.

Chapter 1. Fire in the Skies: January 17, 1991

1. Rick Atkinson, *Crusade: The Untold Story of the Persian Gulf War* (New York: Houghton Mifflin Company, 1993), p. 35.

2. Paul F. Crickmore and Alison J. Crickmore, *F-117 Nighthawk* (Osceola, Wis.: MBI Publishing Company, 1999), p. 108.

3. Atkinson, p. 17.

4. Ibid., p. 19.

5. Richard Mackenzie, "Apache Attack," *Air Force—Journal of the Air Force Association*, October 1991, vol. 74, no. 10.

Chapter 2. Prelude to War: A History of Iraq

1. Borgna Brunner, ed., *The Time Almanac 2002* (Boston: Information Please, 2001), p. 789.

Chapter 3. The Buildup: Operation Desert Shield

1. Robert F. Dorr, *Desert Shield, The Build-up: The Complete Story* (Osceola, Wis.: Motorbooks International, 1991), p. 99.

2. Ibid.

3. Ibid., p. 125.

4. Ibid., p. 119.

Chapter 4. The Battle: Operation Desert Storm

1. William Arkin, "Masterminding an Air War," *Washington Post: Fog of War, 1998*, <http://www.washingtonpost.com/ wp-srv/inatl/longterm/fogofwar/wargoals.htm> (February 20, 2002).

2. H. Rhoads, "Activism Revives on Campus," *Progressive*, March 1991, vol. 55, Issue 3, p. 15.

3. Jerry Adler, "Prayers and Protest," *Newsweek*, January 28, 1991, vol. 117, p. 36.

4. Rick Atkinson, "Crusade: The Untold Story of the Persian Gulf War," *Washington Post: Fog of War, 1993*, <http://www.washingtonpost.com/wp-srv/inatl/longterm/fogofwar/index/crusade.htm> (February 20, 2002).

5. "Scud War, Round Two," *Air Force—Journal of the Air Force Association*, April 1992, <http://www.afa.org/magazine/perspectives/desert_storm/0492scud.html>.

6. The United States Department of Defense, *DefenseLINK News: The Operation Desert Shield/Desert Storm Timeline*, May 16, 2002, <www.defenselink.mil/news/Aug2000/n08082000_20008088.html>.

7. *Desert Storm: The War in the Persian Gulf* (New York: Time Warner Publishing, 1991), p. 202.

8. T. M. Hawley, *Against the Fires of Hell: The Environmental Disaster of the Gulf War* (New York: Harcourt, Brace and Jovanovich, 1992), p. 183.

9. *Desert Storm: The War in the Persian Gulf,* p. 202.

10. Lawrence Freedman and Efraim Karsh, *The Gulf Conflict 1990–1991* (Princeton: Princeton University Press, 1993), p. 402.

11. Ibid., p. 401.

12. Ibid., p. 402.

13. Ibid., p. 408.

14. PBS, "Trainor on the Iraqi Death Toll," *Frontline: The Gulf War*, 2001, <http://www.pbs.org/wgbh/pages/frontline/gulf/appendix/tdeath.html> (February 20, 2002).

Chapter 5. Cease-fire and Aftermath

1 George Bush, "Address to the Nation on the Suspension of Allied Offensive Combat Operations in the Persian Gulf," February 27, 1991, <http://bushlibrary.tamu.edu/papers/1991/91022702.html> (February 20, 2002).

2. Lawrence Freedman and Efraim Karsh, *The Gulf Conflict 1990–1991* (Princeton: Princeton University Press, 1993), p. 412.

3. George Bush and Brent Scowcroft, "Why we didn't remove Saddam," *Time Canada*, March 2, 1998, vol. 151, p. 25.

4. "Who Really Won the War?" *Washington Post/ABC News poll*, n.d., <http://www.vfw.org/magazine/jan01/12.html> (February 20, 2002).

5. Andy Walton, "Of Feminism and Foxholes: Military, Civilian Leaders Reconsider the Role of Women in Combat," *CNN.com*, 2001, <http://www.cnn.com/SPECIALS/2001/gulf.war/legacy/women/> (February 20, 2002).

6. Joellen Perry, "Rhonda Cornum," *U.S. News & World Report*, August 20, 2001, p. 30.

7. Rhonda Cornum, *She Went to War: The Rhonda Cornum Story* (Novato, Calif.: Presidio Press, 1993), p. 10.

8. Ibid., p. 12.

9. PBS, "War Stories," *Frontline: The Gulf War*, 2001, <http://www.pbs.org/wgbh/pages/frontline/gulf/war> (February 20, 2002).

10. Ibid.

11. *Army Times*, April 19, 1999, vol. 59, Issue 38, p. 2.

12. Perry, p. 30.

13. Cornum, p. 137.

14. Department of Veterans Affairs, *Office of Public Affairs News Service*, "VA Fact Sheet—Illnesses of Gulf War Veterans," April 2000, <http://www.va.gov>.

15. Somini Sengupta, "U.N. Broadens List of Products Iraq Can Import," *The New York Times*, May 15, 2002.

Further Reading

Bratman, Fred. *War in the Persian Gulf.* Brookfield, Conn.: The Millbrook Press, 1991.

Deegan, Paul J. *Operation Desert Storm.* Edina, Minn.: ABDO Publishing Company, 1991.

Foster, Leila Merrell. *The Story of the Persian Gulf War.* Chicago: Children's Press, 1991.

Kent, Zachary. *The Persian Gulf War: "The Mother of All Battles."* Berkeley Heights, N.J.: Enslow Publishers, Inc., 1994.

Landau, Elaine. *Colin Powell: Four Star General.* Danbury, Conn.: Franklin Watts, 1991.

Langley, Wanda. *The Air Force in Action.* Berkeley Heights, N.J.: Enslow Publishers, Inc., 2001.

Nardo, Don. *The Persian Gulf War.* San Diego: Lucent Books, 1991.

Valentine, E. J. H. *Norman Schwarzkopf.* New York: Bantam Books, 1991.

Wolkovits, John F. *The Persian Gulf War: Leaders and Generals.* San Diego: Lucent Books, 2001.

Index